BATS AND THEIR YOUNG

BY

PROF. BURT G. WILDER

ISBN-13:
978-1727162752

ISBN-10:
1727162757

EXCEPTING the colder regions, all parts of the world are inhabited by bats. There are many kinds, and they often occur in very large numbers. Probably there are very few persons, young or old, who have not seen a bat. Yet, aside from professed naturalists, it is equally probable that there are still fewer who, from direct observation, could give any accurate description of their appearance or their habits, their structure, or their relations with the "birds of the air," or the "beasts of the earth," to both of which bats bear more or less resemblance.

Nor is this strange; for bats pass the day in caves and deserted buildings, and fly about in pursuit of prey only in the twilight. Much less rapid than that of birds, their flight is so irregular as to render it difficult to follow their course, and in the dusk they are often mistaken for somewhat eccentric members of the swallow family.

Their very aspect is repulsive; they often emit an unpleasant odor; and, worse than all, there is reason for believing them to serve as the vehicle by which the *Cimex lectularius,* that terror of house-keepers, has sometimes

gained entrance to habitations where its
presence would never have been suspected.

When taken they bite so fiercely that we
may be thankful that they are no larger, and
that, as a rule, they prefer insects to human
beings as food. No tiger could be more
violent in its demonstrations or more
capable of using its only weapons, the sharp,
almost needle-like eye-teeth.

This accounts for the rarity of instances of
the domestication of bats, and this, in part,
for the difficulty of making any extended
observations upon them. Having found
recorded but two such cases, I will begin my
account of bats in general with a brief
history of one individual which I succeeded
in taming quite thoroughly. It was when I
was a boy, and the details have escaped me,
but the main facts are as follows:

One of our common bats (probably either
the "little brown bat," *Vespertilio subulatus,*
or the "little red bat") flew into the house
one evening and was caught under a hat. It
squeaked and snapped its little jaws so
viciously that all efforts toward closer
acquaintance were postponed until morning.

When uncovered the next day it seemed as fierce as before, but less active in its movements, probably overpowered by the glare of daylight. When touched its jaws opened wide, the sharp teeth were

FIG. 1.—COMMON ENGLISH BAT (*Vespertilio communis*).

exposed, and from its little throat came the sharp steely clicks so characteristic of our bats. Nor did this fierce demeanor soften in the least daring the day, and when night approached I was about to let it go, but the sight of a big fly upon the window suggested an attempt to feed the captive. Held by the wings between the points of a pair of forceps, the fly had no sooner touched the bat's nose than it was seized, crunched, and swallowed. The rapidity of its disappearance accorded with the width to which the eater's jaws were opened to receive it, and, but for the dismal crackling of skin and wings, reminded one of the sudden engulfment of beetles by a hungry young robin.

A second fly went the same road. The third was more deliberately masticated, and I ventured to pat the devourer's head. Instantly all was changed. The jaws gaped as if they would separate, the crushed fly dropped from the tongue, and the well-known click proclaimed a hatred and defiance which hunger could not subdue nor food appease. So at least it seemed, and I think any but a boy-naturalist would have yielded to the temptation to fling the spiteful creature out of the window. Perhaps, too, a certain obstinacy made me unwilling to so easily relinquish the newly-formed hope of domesticating a bat. At any rate, another fly was presented, and, like the former, dropped the moment my fingers touched the head of the bat. With a third I waited until the bat seemed to be actually swallowing, and unable to either discontinue that process or open its mouth to any extent.[1]

Its rage and perplexity were comical to behold, and, when the fly was really down, it seemed to almost burst with the effort to express its indignation. But this did not prevent it from falling into the same trap again; and, to make a long story short, it finally learned by experience that, while chewing and swallowing were more or less interrupted by snapping at me, both operations were quite compatible with my gentle stroking of its head. And even a bat has brains enough to see the foolishness of losing a dinner in order to resent an unsolicited kindness.

In a few days the bat would take flies from my fingers; although, either from eagerness or because blinded by the light, it too often nipped me sharply in its efforts to seize the victim.

Its voracity was almost incredible. For several weeks it devoured at least fifty house-flies in a day (it was vacation, and my playmates had to assist me), and once disposed of *eighty* between daybreak and sunset.

This bat I kept for more than two months. It would shuffle across the table when I entered the room, and lift up its head for the expected fly. When traveling it was carried in my breast-pocket.

In the fall it died, either from overeating or lack of exercise, for I dared not let it out-of-doors, and it was so apt to injure itself in the rooms that I seldom allowed it to fly.

I should add that it drank frequently and greedily from the tip of a camel's hair pencil.

The following bits of bat biography are from White's "Natural History of Selborne," and the "Annals and Magazine of Natural History:"

"Having caught a lively male specimen of the common 'long-eared bat' (Plecotus auritus) and placed the little fellow in a wire-gauze cage, and inserted a few large flies, he was soon attracted by their buzz, and, pricking up his ears (just as a donkey does), he pounced upon his prey. But, instead of taking it directly into his mouth, he covered it with his body and beat it by aid of its arms, etc., into the bag formed by the interfemoral membrane. He then put his head under his body, withdrew the fly from the bag, and devoured it at leisure.

"This appeared to be always the *modus operandi,* more or less cleverly performed. Several times, when the fly happened to be on the flat surface of the ground, the capture

9

appeared more difficult, and my little friend was, by his exertions, thrown on his back. The tail could then be seen turned round, with its tip and the margin of the membrane pressed against the stomach, forming a capital trap, holding the fly, the captor remaining on his back till he had withdrawn the fly from the bag.

"I had no opportunity of observing the action when the bat was in full flight; but, if the insect was captured a few inches from the side of the cage, the mode was the same! When flying, the interfemoral

FIG. 2.—LONG-EARED ENGLISH BAT (*Plecotus auritus*).

membrane is not extended to a flat surface (and appears not capable of being so stretched), but always preserves a more or less concave form, highly calculated to serve the purposes of a skim-net to capture insects on the wins.

"Occasionally, when the bat was sleepy, sitting at the bottom of the cage, nodding his head, a poor, silly 'blue-bottle fly,' no doubt of tender age, and not read in the natural history of the *Vespertilionidæ*, with the greatest confidence walked quietly under the bat, passing nose, ear, and eyes, without danger; but, immediately he touched the sensitive membrane of the bag, it was closed upon him, and there was no retreat except by being helped out of the difficulty by the teeth of the bat.

"I was much entertained last summer with a tame bat which would take flies out of a person's hand. If you gave it any thing to eat, it brought its wings round before the mouth, hovering and hiding its head in the manner of birds of prey when they feed. The adroitness it showed in shearing off the wings of the flies, which were always rejected, was worthy of observation, and pleased me much. Insects seemed to be most acceptable, though it did not refuse raw flesh when offered. ... I saw it several times confute the vulgar opinion that bats, when down on a flat surface, cannot get on the wing again, by rising with great ease from the floor. ..."

So far, we have contented ourselves with treating of bats simply as such, and without reference to their internal structure, their relationship with other animals, or even their differences among themselves; much less have we approached the deeper questions of their origin and destiny—the probabilities as to their ancestry, and the possibilities as to their more or less remote descendants.

In the same way the astronomer may, for a time, speak of a comet only as a certain well-known celestial phenomenon, which may be as obvious to the unaided vision of the ignorant as to his own. But, sooner or later, he cannot refrain from discussing its chemical and physical condition, its course through space, its relations to other comets and to the stars, and, finally, its probable origin from nebulous matter, and its possible transformation into a world like our own.

The comparison may be carried one step farther. For, to the ignorant and superstitious the sudden apparition of a blazing comet has

12

often been a portent of disaster, while even the intelligent shrink with aversion from the flitting bat, and make comparisons with evil spirits.

FIG. 3.—VAMPIRE-BAT OF SOUTH AMERICA (*Vampirus spectrum*).

It must be admitted that most bats are "uncanny" in their aspect, and unfriendly in disposition; while the legends of blood-thirsty vampires have only too much foundation in fact.

But it is only fair to them (the bat family) to admit that the number of species which thus injure men and the larger animals is very

13

small; and that, while all of our own bats, and most of those of other lands, are fierce devourers of insects, and use their sharp teeth for defense against their captors, there are many kinds, especially the larger (Roussettes, etc.), which live almost wholly upon fruits, and are, moreover, quite good eating themselves. So there should be made a distinction between them as between the venomous and the harmless serpents and the more and the less poisonous spiders.

Perhaps one element of distrust of the bat family arises from their apparent non-conformity to either of the common animal types. The bat seems to be either a bird with hair and teeth, bringing forth its young alive, or a mammal with wings, and the general aspect and habit of a bird. Add to these exceptional features that their attitude, when at rest, is always head downward, and that their legs are so turned outward as to bring the knees behind instead of in front, and we may almost pardon the common dislike of the whole family of bats.

FIG. 4.—FLYING-FOX OR ROUSETTE (*Pteropus rubricollis*)

We may as well state at once that a bat is really a *mammal;* that is, it agrees with moles, rats, sheep, horses, cats, monkeys, and men, in bringing forth its young alive, and nursing them by milk; in having red blood-corpuscles, which contain no nucleus; in being clothed with hair; and in possessing a *corpus callosum,* that is, a band of fibres connecting the two cerebral hemispheres.

There are other anatomical features which link the bats closely with the moles and shrews and hedge-hogs. Indeed, the bat

15

might be described as a flying mole, or the mole as a burrowing bat.

Twenty years ago one of these phrases might have been as acceptable as the other; for they would have implied only an ideal connection between the forms. But now, when the idea of an actual evolution or derivation of widely different forms from me another, or from common stocks, is rapidly becoming the fundamental postulate of all biological research, we are bound to inquire whether one mode of expression is not much more likely to be true than the other.

For the solution of this, as of most such inquiries, we must appeal to embryology, to the study of the development of animals, and of the resemblances between the earlier stages of some and the later stages of others.

Our first object is to confirm the conclusion that bats are mammals rather than birds. And here, strangely enough, we find that the matter of *size,* usually regarded as of little moment in zoological discrimination, becomes of primary importance. All animals, mammals as well as birds, are formed from eggs. An egg, or ovum, is a cell with special endowments, and capable of

16

availing itself of the peculiar conditions under which it is placed, the first of these conditions being the access of the zoösperms of the male. Now, the eggs of all mammals are small, usually microscopic. The human ovum is about $\frac{1}{120}$ of an inch in diameter.

Therefore, although the yolk or essential part of the egg of a humming-bird may be pretty small, it is far larger than the largest mammalian ovum; while that of the ostrich or the *Epyornis* is simply gigantic in comparison.

Now, I am not aware that the ovum of a bat has ever been examined, but there can be doubt of its minuteness as compared with that of any known bird. Fig. 5 shows, of its natural size, the earliest embryo of a bat I have ever heard of. Its length as it lies is much less than that of a humming-bird's egg. Moreover, since the young bird is developed upon the yolk, and the latter remains of considerable size until very near the period of hatching, and since the yolk of our little bat either has been already absorbed or is too minute for detection, it may be considered that it was much smaller than that of birds.

17

Finally, the simple fact that the little bat was taken out of the mother already somewhat advanced in development, is clear proof that it is not a bird.[2]

Aside from the absence of yolk, the form of the smallest embryo, above figured, might not determine its mammalian nature; but the remaining figures, however little some of them may resemble quadrupeds, are evidently not birds. The tail is too long (for any bird excepting the *Archeopteryx*); the muzzle is rounded, the feet have five divisions more or less marked, while no bird has more than four toes; and, although the hands may in some cases resemble a bird's wing, yet here too are five fingers, and the wing is evidently an expansion of the hand itself by the elongation and separation of the fingers, rather than a slender hand with feathers attached to the hinder border as with birds. With the more advanced embryos the prominent ear would be conclusive against their avian nature, and the nostrils, where they show, are not those of birds.

We may, then, dismiss from our minds any anxiety as to whether bats are partly birds and partly mammals, and conclude merely that, upon the essential mammalian structure, there have been superinduced features which enable the bat to fly in the air; these, however, no more making it a bird than the form and habit of the whale and manatee render them fishes.

The second question is, whether bats are to be regarded as the progenitors or the descendants of the moles and shrews; or, to put it more accurately (since the idea of derivation does not imply that living species have descended from other living species, but from similar extinct species or from others which combined features since separated in the two forms), is it probable that the existing bats have been produced from original stocks more nearly resembling the moles or the reverse? That the former is the more probable, is indicated upon three grounds:

1. The bat form is peculiar among mammals, and does not, like the *Ornithorhynchus* and *Echidna,* manifest any *internal* structural affinity with birds. There is a much more marked resemblance to the extinct flying reptiles (*Pterodactyli*), but this is probably one of analogy.

2. The embryo bat resembles the ordinary small mammal; the long fingers, the

persistence of the web between them, and its
continuation from the border of the body
and tail, are features of later appearance.

3. In one embryo (Fig. 9), the thinness and
prolongation of the muzzle as compared
with the lower jaw may be compared with
the elongated snouts of the "star-nosed
mole" and the "elephant shrew."

I have never had the opportunity of
examining the young of moles or shrews.
This would be very desirable, and, one
would think, not difficult to accomplish.

Figs. 5 to 11 are intended chiefly to show
the gradual development of the limbs, so the
other parts are drawn with less detail, and no
attempt is made to elucidate the manner of
formation of the face from the visceral
arches.

The series begins with Fig. 5. Here the body
is simply an elongated mass, longer and
rounded at the head end, and tapering at the
other extremity. It is twisted upon itself, as
is often the case with young embryos. The
yolk-sack and membranes are not well
preserved, and are not shown at all in the
figure. This embryo may be regarded as
quite small for even a bat. The limbs have

20

not appeared, so the tail does not form a
distinct prolongation. (The lower figure is of
natural size; the upper is enlarged five
diameters.)

In Fig. 6 the arm (*ar*) and leg (*pes*) project
as little flat pads from the sides of the body.
There is no sign of subdivision into fingers
and toes, and very little difference between
the two limbs. It is worth

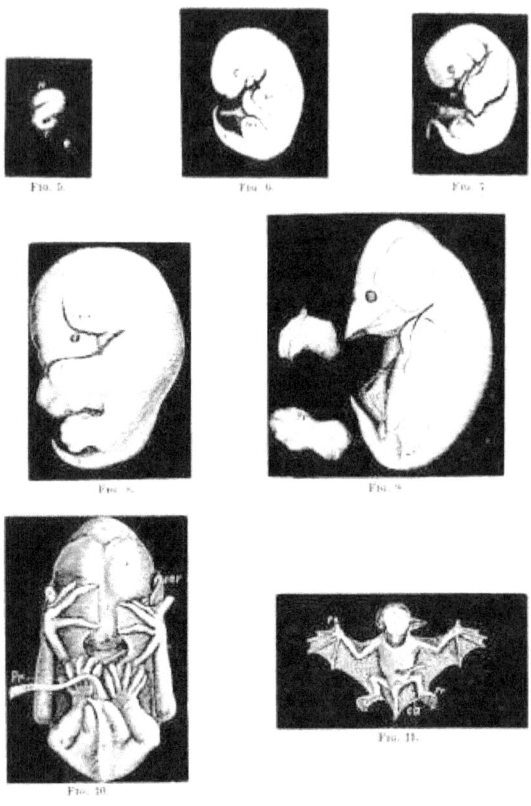

EMBRYO BATS. All, excepting Fig. 11, enlarged 5 diameters.

Explanation of Plate[3]

Figs. 10 and 11 from the little brown bat (*Vespertilio subulatus*), the others from a Brazilian species (*Nyctinomus Brasiliensis*); Fig. 11 and the smaller part of Fig. 5 are of natural size. All the others are enlarged

5 diameters; that is, 25 areas. The lettering is uniform, as follows: *u c,* umbilical cord; not seen in 5 or 8. *H,* head; *T,* tail ; *Ar,* armus or anterior limb; *Pes,* foot; *P,* pollex or thumb, the anterior digit of the manus; *Pr,* primus or great-toe, the anterior dactyl of the pes, which becomes the *outer* in the older bats, but is the *inner* with most animals; *W,* web, the fold of skin which connects the digits with each other and with the leg and margin of the trunk; *C,* calcar, a spur-like process from the heel, serving to extend the web which reaches between the legs and the tail; *Ear,* the ear; in Fig. 7 *H* is the heart; in Fig. 10 *A* is the rounded prominence corresponding to the cerebral hemispheres which are developed from the anterior cerebral vesicle; *M* represents the optic lobes, formed from the middle vesicle; *N,* nostril; *Mo,* mouth; *E,* elbow; *K,* knee. For further explanation, see the text.

noting, however, that the manus is already a little the wider and more prominent.

In Fig. 7 the manus is not only larger but has protruded so as to display the wrist and elbow regions, and a slight prominence upon the anterior border marks the position of the thumb (pollex). In these three specimens I have not as yet found the ear, but in 3 and 4 the eye is quite apparent.

In Fig. 6 the ear is a triangular flap, as in most early mammalian embryos.[4]

The manus and pes have enlarged and present shaded portions corresponding with the thinner tissue between the finger and toes. In the former this is to become the web; in the latter it is wholly removed so as to leave the toes free. The muzzle is partly covered by the manus, but it is already somewhat pointed, as in the next figure.

In Fig. 9 the manus and pes of the left side are shown as if removed from the trunk, so as to expose the flat and prominent muzzle. The ear is a large flap, but still projects forward so as to cover the opening. The pollex has separated from the other digits, and the latter are elongated and bent downward. The pes is longer and the signs of subdivision more distinct. A web connected the limbs and the trunk as in the older specimens, but it was somewhat torn, so that the exact extent could not be determined, and I preferred to wait for a better specimen to show it.

The specimens above described were taken from a Brazilian species, *Nyctinomus Brasiliensis* (which is also found in this country). Figs. 10 and 11 were from the common "little brown bat" (*Vespertllio subulatus*). As might be expected, the increasing limbs are packed about the body

24

more or less irregularly. But in Fig. 10 the limbs of the two sides are placed with almost exact symmetry so as to cover the face and the body. One eye is covered, the other peeps out over the index-finger. The ears are firmly held down by the thumbs, and one of the nostrils is partly hidden by the web. The lower part of the trunk and the tail are bent upward, and the knees are thrown outward so as to bring the great-toe (*pr*) upon the outer instead of the inner side. The whole suggests an effort upon the part of the embryo to not only occupy the least possible space, but also to screen itself from observation, and neither see, nor hear, nor smell.

In Fig. 11 is shown an older embryo, of natural size, outspread so as to display the characteristic features of bats; the greatly-elongated fingers; the separation of the thumb; and the extension of the web, with the reticulated arrangement of vessels and nerves upon it. This nervous expansion seems to enable bats to perceive the proximity of bodies by the change in the pressure of the air.

THE SIZE OF BAT FAMILIES.—It is not known that bats make a nest like birds, or that they have any other way of caring for their young than by carrying them hanging to their fur whether during flight or while suspended at rest by the legs.

So we might naturally infer two things: first, that the young bats would be born in a somewhat advanced condition so as to be able as soon as possible to shift for themselves; and, second, that the number produced at a birth would be small.

The former inference would seem to be true, judging from the large size of the little bats before birth, and the rarity of the capture of the mothers with young. In one case the two unborn young weighed two-thirds as much as the parent, and the average of twenty individuals gave the weight of the young as four-tenths that of the parents.

Upon the second point it is stated by Van der Hoeven ("Handbook of Zoölogy," vol. ii., p. 731) that "bats commonly produce one or two young ones at a birth;" but he does not say upon how many observations the conclusion is based.

Prof. Owen ("Comparative Anatomy of Vertebrates," vol. iii., p. 730) Records two observations of bats (*Vespertilio emarginatus* and *V. noctula*), with each one

young, and concludes that this is commonly
the case with all bats.

A collared fruit bat (*Cynonycteris collaris*)
produced a single young February 27, 1870,
and a second April 7, 1871.[5]

In Jamaica Mr. Osborn observed several
females of *Molossus fumarius* and
Monophyllus poeyi, with each one young.[6]

The same observer mentions two other
species (*Macrotus Waterhousii,* and
Monophyllus Redmanii), without specifying
the number of young; but we may infer that,
as in the other cases, each female had but
one.

In a single female of an undetermined
Brazilian species I have found one young;
and in each of forty females of the
Nyctinomus Brasiliensis (from Brazil) a
single young.

These are certainly facts in corroboration of
the opinions of Owen and Van der Hoeven,
but let us not be hasty in generalizing from
them respecting all bats.

In June, 1874, there were brought to me
twenty females of the "little brown bat"

27

(*Vespertilio subulatus*). Each was found to contain two little bats in various stages of development.[7]

Finally, Prof. Putnam, of the Peabody Academy of Science, has kindly allowed me to examine two females of the *Lasiurus novehoracensis* taken in Massachusetts, on each of which were three young bats.

The foregoing observations indicate that, while one is the more common number of young produced by bats, two and three may occur. More extended inquiry may show that these larger families are less rare than now appears, and even that as many as four young may be produced at a birth. For while bats are usually credited with only two nipples, an extra pair exists upon the *Lasiurus noveboracensis*.

The uniformity in number with each species is very striking. Twenty-two of one species had each two young, while forty of another had each one.

In the former case the young were placed one on the right and the other on the left of the body. But in the latter case the single young was invariably on the right side; while, in the single specimen of the

undetermined Brazilian bat, the young was
on the left side.

Equally striking with the above facts is the
isolation of the females with young. Among
forty-three *Nyctinomus Brasiliensis* was but
a single male. No males were found near the
twenty-two *Vespertilio suhulatus.* Osborn
says that, of *Molossus fumarius,* all of one
large lot were males; while at another time,
in a large hollow tree, he found in one cavity
about one hundred males, and in a second
about the same number of females, with
"apparently a few males here and there."

Evidently there is much to be learned
respecting the domestic and social economy
of these animals. Perhaps the males gather
food for the females.[8]

Perhaps the most important fact, from a
practical point of view, is that of the power
of the mother-bats to carry such a weight of
young in addition to their own. Yet, so far as
I know, all estimates of the extent of wing
and size of muscle, which would be
necessary to enable a man to fly, have been
based upon the idea that the only flying
mammal is a fair standard.[9]

These estimates should be corrected so as to conform to the fact that a bat can fly with nearly double its ordinary weight. Even this may not encourage us to hope for a future race of flying-men. But it renders it worth considering whether a man, naturally slight of frame, with small head, could not so far reduce his weight by a flesh diet, and by the amputation of his legs, as to enable him, by special cultivation of his pectoral muscles, to work effectively a pair of wings less extensive than those now supposed to be required.

1.

• I did not understand this at the time. If my readers will try it, they will find that it is very difficult to even begin to swallow with the mouth open, and almost impossible to prevent the morsel from descending after reaching the back of the throat.

• There are no known birds which normally produce living young; but I have a chicken-like body nearly three inches long, which was developed within the hen. It was shown at the meeting of the American Association for the Advancement of Science, this year. Its exact nature can only be learned after full examination of the structure.

- Figs. 5 to 11 were all drawn and engraved from nature by Mr. Philip Barnard.
- It remains to be seen whether the seals, whales, manatee, and dugong, have a pinna in the earlier stages, and afterward lose it. Upon the earliest embryo of a manatee yet known, see a paper by the writer in *American Journal of Science,* August, 1875.
- P. L. Sclater, "Proceedings of Zoölogical Society, 1870, 1871."
- "Proceedings of Zoölogical Society, 1865," p. 81.
- I have since seen a bat of another species, to which were clinging two young.
- The writer has not been able to examine the development of bats with the nasal appendages. He would be glad to receive information upon the habits of bats with young, and to exchange the latter for specimens of *Amphioxus.*

9. - Harting ("Archives Néerlandisches," iv.) calculated that a bat the size of a man would require wings two and a half metres long, and with a surface of one and a half square metre.

* 9 7 8 1 7 2 7 1 6 2 7 5 2 *